# SANJEEV KAPOOR
# CHAAT

Published by
POPULAR PRAKASHAN PVT. LTD.
301, Mahalaxmi Chambers
22, Bhulabhai Desai Road
Mumbai - 400 026
for Khana Khazana Publications Pvt. Ltd.

© 2008 Sanjeev Kapoor
First Published 2008
Second Reprint 2014

(4158)
ISBN – 978-81-7991-411-3

Design: Quadrant Infotech (India) Pvt. Ltd
Photography: Bharat Bhirangi

PRINTED IN INDIA
by Infinity Advertising Services Pvt. Ltd.
D – 4/2, Okhla Industrial Area Phase-1
New Delhi 110020

# SANJEEV KAPOOR
# CHAAT

In Association with Alyona Kapoor

Popular Prakashan

www.popularprakashan.com

*Chaat*! Just the mention of this word sets everyone's taste buds watering including mine!! I spent my childhood in Meerut where we would frequent Cantonment Road which is famous for the *chaat*. We used to simply gorge on them, the taste of which still lingers in my memory.

*Chaat* is very close to what Indian food generally is – *chatpata*! It is a scrumptious blend of *teekha*, *meetha*, *khatta*, *namkeen* – absolutely tasty. The word '*chaat*' is derived from the Hindi verb '*chaatna*' which literally means 'to lick one's fingers cle Served cold and sometimes even hot it is a versatile any-time snack.

There was a time when *chaat* was an important part of the street foods mostly in Delhi, Uttar Pradesh, Rajasthan, Gujarat, Bihar, Meerut, Indore and Kolkata. People enjoy the *chaat* from Indore so much so that it has become an integral part of the menus offered by well-known caterers. Even in restaurants you will find a variety of *Chaat* displayed prominently on the menu cards. And now varieties of *chaat* are found in plentiful across the length and breadth of India. Wherever you go you get *chaat* with, naturally, the local touch.

But hygiene is an issue when it comes to partaking of *chaat* sold on the street corners. This has made some people a little wary. These days I often see little bill boards saying '*Paani Puri* with mineral water' – perhaps a last ditch effort to retair their patrons.

h *chaat* being such a favourite snack in most homes, where both young and old
oy them with equal pleasure, it would be a rewarding experience to prepare them
nome. This way one can not only assure hygiene but also good value for money. If
are very fond of *chaat*, you may even make a meal of it occasionally.

s was the foremost thought when I planned this book. As the flavours of black
:, cumin and chutneys begin to seep out from within the covers of this book, you
find a plethora of well-researched *chaat* recipes – with a sprinkling of fusion to
that extra tang. Savour a cocktail of seasonal fruits in *Fruit Chaat* or enjoy a
olesome *Baby Uttappa* with *Aloo Bhaji*, or better still gorge on a *Chinese Bhel*…
ısual but tasty, they are all winners all the way! Try out these recipes a couple
imes to gain confidence and then you can be confident that you will be able to
ertain your guests to a 'chat and *chaat* party'. And then who knows… maybe start
ır own '*chaat*' business.

ppy cooking!!

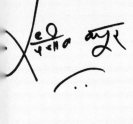

# acknowledgements

heen Panjwani

pa Das

wini Patwardhan

arati Anand

artendu Sharma

pal Singh Sokhi

tsna & Mayur Dvivedi

hendra Ghanekar

. Lata Lohana & Capt. K. K. Lohana

nrata & Sanjiv Bahl

ena Murdeshwar

a & Rajeev Kapoor

eev Matta

a D'Souza

jay Thorat

rabh Mishra

pa Rane

eeta Bhatkal

ta Bhagattjee

ayak Gawande

# Contents

# ALOO ANAARDANA CHAAT

*The bejeweled look of this chaat is a sight to behold.*

*And its superb taste will have everyone asking for more!*

## Ingredients

2 large potatoes, boiled and cut into 1-inch pieces

1 cup pomegranate kernels

1 large onion, chopped

2 green chillies, chopped

½ cup roasted peanuts

2 tablespoons chopped fresh coriander leaves

1 tablespoon chopped fresh mint leaves

2 teaspoons *chaat masala*

Salt to taste

½ cup *sev*

1 teaspoon lemon juice

2 tablespoons Green Coriander Chutney (page 100)

## Method

1. In a large bowl, combine the potatoes, pomegranate, onion, green chillies, peanuts, coriander leaves, mint leaves, *chaat masala* and salt and toss well to mix.

2. Add the *sev*, lemon juice and green coriander chutney and toss again.

3. Transfer the mixture to individual bowls and serve immediately.

# AMERICAN SEV PURI

*'Canapés with corn salsa' could be another name for this dish!*
*But trick or treat, this makes a great starter at any party.*

## Ingredients

1 cup American sweet corn, boiled

½ cup *sev*

24 canapé cases

1 tablespoon oil + for deep-frying

1 medium onion, chopped

2 fresh red chillies, chopped

¼ cup sweet chilli sauce

½ teaspoon *chaat masala*

1 tablespoon chopped fresh mint leaves

2 tablespoons chopped fresh coriander leaves

1 tablespoon lemon juice

2 tablespoons chopped fresh parsley

## Method

1. Heat one tablespoon of oil in a pan; add the onion and sauté for a while. Add the
   and sauté for a few minutes. Add the red chillies and sweet chilli sauce and toss to
   Add the *chaat masala*, mint leaves and coriander leaves. Mix and cook till dry.
2. Heat the oil in a *kadai* and deep-fry the canapés lightly, taking care that they do not b
   Drain well on absorbent paper. Set aside to cool.
3. Add the lemon juice to the corn mixture and mix well. Spoon into the canapés and spri
   with *sev*. Garnish with parsley and serve immediately.

# BABY UTTAPPA WITH ALOO BHAJI

*Look on this as a desi pizza because the cheese topping makes it so!*
*Try this at your kid's birthday party and rest assured the children will love it!*

## Ingredients

2 cups ready-mixed *uttappam* batter

Oil as required

½ cup *aloo bhaji*

8 tablespoons grated mozzarella cheese

2 teaspoons Red Chilli-Garlic Chutney (page 101)

4 teaspoons Green Coriander Chutney (page 100)

4 teaspoons Date and Tamarind Chutney (page 102)

6 tablespoons *sev*

## Method

1. Heat a non-stick *tawa* and grease it lightly. For each *uttappa*, pour one ladleful of b
   onto the *tawa* and spread with the back of the ladle to make a moderately thick three
   round *uttappa*. Drizzle some oil all around.

2. Spread a little *aloo bhaji* on top and cook till the base is pale gold.

3. Sprinkle mozzarella cheese over the *bhaji*, cover the pan and cook till the ch
   melts.

4. Turn out the *uttappa* onto a serving plate. Spread all the three chutneys over the
   sprinkle *sev* and serve immediately. Make the remaining *uttappa* in the same way.

# BHAKARWADI CHAAT

*This calls for some fine tuning between the crispiness of the bhakarwadi and
the great absorption power of yogurt and chutneys.
But I never worry about these things as a chaat is a chaat is a chaat... make it whichever way!*

## Ingredients

1 cup mini *bhakarwadi*

½ cup bean (*moong*) sprouts

1 cup yogurt

Salt to taste

2 medium potatoes, boiled and finely chopped

1 large onion, finely chopped

5 tablespoons Green Coriander Chutney (page 100)

3 tablespoons Date and Tamarind Chutney (page 102)

1 teaspoon *chaat masala*

¼ teaspoon red chilli powder

1 teaspoon roasted cumin powder

¼ cup nylon *sev*

2 tablespoons chopped fresh coriander leaves

## Method

1.  Cook the bean sprouts in one and a half cups of boiling salted water for two or t
    minutes. Drain, refresh in cold water and set aside.
2.  Whisk yogurt with salt and place in a refrigerator to chill for half an hour.
3.  To prepare the *chaat*, arrange the *bhakarwadi* in a large serving plate; top with laye
    *moong* sprouts, potatoes, onion and chilled yogurt.
4.  Drizzle both the chutneys and sprinkle *chaat masala*, chilli powder, cumin powder
    nylon *sev* over the yogurt.
5.  Garnish with coriander leaves and serve immediately.

# BHEL PURI

*Take a few humble ingredients and jumble them up with chutneys.*
*What you get is the signature street food of Mumbai! With this recipe, bring home that same magic but make loads of it because no one stops at one serving!*

## Ingredients

2 cups puffed rice (*kurmura*)

1 medium onion, chopped

¼ cup roasted *masala chana dal*

¼ cup roasted peanuts

2 medium potatoes, boiled, peeled and diced

2-3 green chillies, chopped

½ cup *sev*

8 crisp *puris*

Salt to taste

¼ cup Green Coriander Chutney (page 100)

½ cup Date and Tamarind Chutney (page 102)

2 tablespoons Red Chilli-Garlic Chutney (page 101)

1 teaspoon lemon juice

2 tablespoons chopped fresh coriander leaves

## Method

1.  Combine the puffed rice, onion, *chana dal*, peanuts, potatoes, green chillies and half the *sev* in a bowl and toss well to mix.
2.  Add four crushed *puris* and salt to taste and mix again.
3.  Add the chutneys to taste and the lemon juice and mix well.
4.  Garnish with coriander leaves and the remaining *sev*. Serve immediately with remaining *puris*.

# BHUNA BHUTTA

*Corn on the cob on charcoal. Get the aroma?*

*Slather with lemon and take a deep breath… transports me straight back to my childhood days when corn (or challi in Punjabi) would be a must on a rainy day.*

## Ingredients

2 American corn cobs (*bhutta*)

Salt to taste

2 tablespoons butter

2 tablespoons lemon juice

1 teaspoon red chilli flakes

1 teaspoon red chilli powder

2 teaspoons brown sugar

## Method

1. Remove the husks of the corn.
2. Place each cob on a twelve-inch square piece of aluminium foil.
3. Either sprinkle with salt and brush with butter and lemon juice, or sprinkle salt, chilli flakes, chilli powder and brown sugar, and brush with butter and lemon juice.
4. Wrap the aluminium foil around the cobs and twist the ends as for a toffee. Place on live charcoals or on a grill and cook for fifteen minutes.
5. Open the foil wrapping and serve hot.

# BISCUIT CORN SEV PURI

*Talk about a large and strong foundation!*
*The cream crackers hold the toppings pretty well.*
*I recommend this dish for those who don't like fragile puris.*

## Ingredients

16 cream cracker biscuits

2 large potatoes, boiled and mashed

½ cup corn kernels, blanched

Salt to taste

¼ teaspoon red chilli powder

2 medium onions, chopped

*Chaat masala* as required

8–10 teaspoons Green Coriander Chutney (page 100)

2 tablespoons Red Chilli-Garlic Chutney (page 101)

8–10 teaspoons Date and Tamarind Chutney (page 102)

1 cup fine *sev*

2 tablespoons chopped fresh coriander leaves

1 small unripe green mango, chopped

## Method

1.  Arrange four biscuits on each plate.
2.  In a separate bowl, mix together the mashed potatoes, corn, salt and chilli powder. D
    into sixteen portions. Place a portion of the potato mixture on each biscuit. Sprinkle c
    and *chaat masala* on top.
3.  Drizzle half a teaspoon of green coriander chutney, one-fourth teaspoon of red chilli-ξ
    chutney and one teaspoon of date and tamarind chutney one over the other on
    biscuit. Cover the biscuits with plenty of *sev*.
4.  Sprinkle coriander leaves and green mango on top. Serve immediately.

**Chef's Tip:** Add more red chilli-garlic chutney for a spicier snack.

# CANAPÉS WITH CHOLE

*Chole is wonderful with chutney. And if enhanced with yogurt, it makes wonderful comfort food.*
*You can use leftover chole too and turn it into something special!*

## Ingredients

16 canapé cases, fried

1½ cups yogurt, whisked and chilled

1 teaspoon red chilli powder

2 teaspoons roasted cumin powder

2 teaspoons *chaat masala*

¼ cup Green Coriander Chutney
  (page 100)

### Chole

1 cup chickpeas (*kabuli chana*), soaked

Salt to taste

2 teaspoons tea leaves

2 tablespoons *ghee*

2 medium onions, chopped

1 teaspoon ginger paste

1 teaspoon garlic paste

4 tablespoons *chole masala*

¾ cup fresh tomato purée

4 tablespoons chopped fresh coriand
  leaves

## Method

1. To make the *chole*, place the chickpeas with three cups of water and salt in a pres
   cooker. Tie up the tea leaves in a piece of muslin to make a *potli;* add to the chickp
   Close the lid and cook till the pressure is released five to six times (five to six whistle
   till the chickpeas are soft. Discard the *potli.* Drain and set aside. Reserve one-fourth
   of stock for cooking.

2. Heat two tablespoons of *ghee* in a *kadai;* add the onions and sauté over a low hea
   light golden. Add the ginger paste and garlic paste and sauté for half a minute.

3. Add three tablespoons of *chole masala* and continue to sauté for another minute.
   the tomato purée and cook over a low heat for two to three minutes.

4. Add the boiled chickpeas and the reserved stock and simmer for five minutes, or till a
   water is absorbed and the *ghee* rises to the surface. Sprinkle the remaining *chole ma*
   and coriander leaves, stir and cover immediately. Remove from heat and keep warm

5. Place canapés on individual serving plates. Fill each canapé with two to three tablesp
   of prepared *chole*. Pour some whisked yogurt over and sprinkle a little chilli pow
   roasted cumin powder and *chaat masala*. Finally drizzle a little green coriander chu
   on each canapé and serve immediately.

# CHATPATI SHANKERPALI

*If I had a chance to talk about creative chaats at length, I would talk about this shankerpali medley*
*But why waste time discussing things... try out this chaat and savour the crunch for yourself.*

## Ingredients

2 cups savoury *shankerpali*, crushed

1 large onion, chopped

1 large tomato, seeded and chopped

3 green chillies, chopped

1 small unripe green mango, chopped

¼ cup *masala chana dal*

½ cup *tikha sev*

3 tablespoons chopped fresh coriander leaves

4 teaspoons Green Coriander Chutney (page 100)

1½ tablespoons Date and Tamarind Chutney (page 102)

1 teaspoon lemon juice

Salt to taste

## Method

1.  In a large bowl, combine the crushed *shankerpali*, onion, tomato, green chillies, gr
    mango, *masala chana dal* and *tikha sev* and toss to mix well.

2.  Add the coriander leaves, green coriander chutney, date and tamarind chutney, ler
    juice and salt and toss again.

3.  Spoon into four individual bowls and serve immediately.

# CHINESE BHEL

*When we talk about fusion food, this bhel is top of the chaats!*
*Fairly easy to make, ensure that it is served as soon the sauces touch the crispy noodles.*

## Ingredients

200 grams eggless noodles

Salt to taste

Oil for deep-frying

2–3 spring onions, sliced

½ cup bean (*moong*) sprouts

¼ cup roasted peanuts, crushed

1 tablespoon Sichuan sauce

1 tablespoon tomato ketchup

Sliced spring onion greens, to garnish

## Method

1. Cook the noodles in six to eight cups of boiling salted water, to which one tablespoon oil has been added, till almost done. Drain, refresh in cold water, drain again and spread on a large plate to cool.

2. Heat the oil in a wok and deep-fry noodles till crisp and golden brown. Drain on absorbent paper and leave to cool. Lightly crush the fried noodles.

3. In a large bowl, combine the crushed noodles, spring onions, bean sprouts and peanuts and toss to mix.

4. Add the Sichuan sauce and tomato ketchup and toss the mixture once more. Adjust seasoning.

5. Serve in individual plates, garnished with spring onion greens.

# DABELI

*There is something about this sandwich that makes it so endearing: that something is the masala perhaps, or the crunch of the peanuts, or the punch of the chutneys... I think you will find out for yourself!*

## Ingredients

4 pav

1½ tablespoons *dabeli masala* powder

3 tablespoons oil

2 large potatoes, boiled, peeled and mashed

Salt to taste

1 teaspoon lemon juice

1 cup Date and Tamarind Chutney (page 102)

1 tablespoon sugar

½ cup spiced peanuts (*masala moongphali*)

¼ cup grated fresh coconut

¼ cup fresh pomegranate kernels

10–12 black grapes, chopped

1 cup nylon *sev*

2 tablespoons fresh coriander leaves, chopped

¼ cup Red Chilli-Garlic Chutney (page 101)

2 medium onions, finely chopped

2 tablespoons butter

## Method

1. Heat the oil in a pan; add the potato, salt and a little water. Mix well and add the *dabeli masala*, lemon juice, a quarter cup of date and tamarind chutney and sugar. Mix and cook till quite dry.

2. Spread the mixture on a plate. Sprinkle *masala* peanuts, grated coconut, pomegranate, black grapes, half the sev and coriander leaves on top.

3. Slit the *pavs* horizontally without cutting through. Spread the red chilli-garlic chutney, a layer each of the potato stuffing, tamarind chutney, onion and *sev* in between the two halves.

4. Place the stuffed *pav* on a hot *tawa*. Press lightly, spread with a little butter and toast on both sides, till heated through and slightly crisp. Serve hot.

# DAHI BATATA PURI

*If you have some puris left over after a paani puri binge, serve them up stuffed with potatoes and sprouts. And believe me, not a single soul in the house will complain!*

## Ingredients

24 crisp puffed *puris* (as for *paani puri*)

1½ cups yogurt, whisked

Salt to taste

1 tablespoon sugar

2 medium potatoes, boiled and chopped

½ cup sprouted *moong*, blanched

1 teaspoon red chilli powder

½ teaspoon *chaat masala*

¼ cup Green Coriander Chutney (page 100)

¼ cup Date and Tamarind Chutney (page 102)

*Sev*, as required

1 teaspoon roasted cumin powder

2 tablespoons chopped fresh coriander leaves

2 tablespoons pomegranate kernels

## Method

1.  Add salt and sugar to the yogurt and whisk till smooth. Place in a refrigerator till ready to use.
2.  Mix together the boiled potatoes, sprouted *moong*, salt, half a teaspoon of chilli powder and *chaat masala*.
3.  Make a hole in each *puri*, fill with the potato filling, dip in the yogurt and place on a plate. Alternatively, place the *puris* on the plate and pour the yogurt over, reserving a little for the topping.
4.  Place dollops of the green coriander chutney and date and tamarind chutney over the yogurt. Sprinkle the *sev*, remaining chilli powder, roasted cumin powder, coriander leaves and pomegranate over the *puris*, and finally top with the remaining yogurt.
5.  Serve immediately.

# DAHI BHALLE

*Dahi Bhalle are perfect with Chole Bhature and this combo is a sure
thing at a formal dinner in a Punjabi home... I know because I have grown up on this staple die*

## Ingredients

¾ cup split black gram (*dhuli urad dal*)

Salt to taste

15–20 raisins (*kishmish*)

1 inch ginger, chopped

2 green chillies, chopped

2 tablespoons gram flour (*besan*)

Oil for deep-frying

4–5 cups yogurt

1 teaspoon rock salt (*sendha namak*

1 tablespoon sugar

Green Coriander Chutney (page 10(
  as required

Date and Tamarind Chutney (page 1
  as required

2 teaspoons roasted cumin powder

2 tablespoons chopped fresh
  coriander leaves

## Method

1. Wash and soak the *dal* in three cups of cold water overnight. Drain excess wat
   following day and grind the *dal* to a smooth paste.

2. Add the salt, raisins, ginger, green chillies and gram flour to the batter and whisk f
   minutes to make a fluffy batter.

3. Heat the oil in a *kadai*. Drop the batter in tablespoonfuls into the hot oil and fry the
   until light golden.

4. Drain the *bhalle* and soak in plenty of water for two minutes. Squeeze betweer
   palms to drain out water.

5. Whisk the yogurt well with rock salt and sugar to taste.

6. To serve, place *bhalle* on a plate and cover with yogurt. Drizzle green coriander ch
   and date and tamarind chutney on top and sprinkle with roasted cumin powder.

7. Garnish with coriander leaves and serve immediately.

**Chef's Tip**: You can stuff the *bhalle* with a mixture of raisins, crushed cashew nuts and chop
coriander leaves to make Kalmi Wade. In which case, do not add raisins to the *urad dal* ba

# DHOKLA CHAAT

*I find it extremely convenient to buy ready–made dhoklas and douse them with the yogurt and chutn*
*This little recipe is a saviour when you have unexpected guests who want a heavy snack.*

## Ingredients

500 grams *khaman dhokla*, cut into 1½-inch cubes

1½ cups skimmed milk yogurt, whisked

3 tablespoons Green Coriander Chutney (page 100)

3 tablespoons Date and Tamarind Chutney (page 102)

*Sev* as required

4 tablespoons chopped fresh coriander leaves

## Method

1. Place the *dhokla* in a large serving dish. Pour the yogurt over and drizzle with the chutneys.

2. Sprinkle *sev* generously on top and serve immediately, garnished with coriander le

# DILLI ALOO KACHALU CHAAT

*Combine full–bodied tubers with the tanginess of chutneys and pickled ginger.*

## Ingredients

2 large potatoes, cut into 1-inch pieces

1 large sweet potato, cut into 1-inch pieces

1 inch ginger, cut into thin strips

2 teaspoons lemon juice

Salt to taste

Oil for shallow-frying

1 tablespoon Date and Tamarind Chutney (page 102)

1 teaspoon *chaat masala*

½ teaspoon red chilli powder

2 teaspoons roasted cumin powder

2 green chillies, chopped

3 tablespoons chopped fresh coriander leaves

## Method

1.  Place the ginger in a small bowl; add one teaspoon of lemon juice and a pinch of salt well and chill in a refrigerator till ready to use.

2.  Heat the oil on a thick *tawa* till moderately hot. Add the potatoes and shallow-fry till and golden. Drain on absorbent paper.

3.  To the same oil, add the sweet potato and shallow-fry till crisp and golden. Drai absorbent paper.

4.  Transfer the potatoes and sweet potatoes to a large bowl. Add the salt, date and tam chutney, *chaat masala*, chilli powder, cumin powder, green chillies, coriander leaves the remaining lemon juice and mix well.

5.  To serve, transfer the mixture to a serving bowl, garnish with ginger strips and serve immediately.

# DILLI ALOO TIKKI CHAAT

*Plump stuffed tikkis dunked in wholesome pea curry... this is one snack you can convert into a mini meal!*

## Ingredients

### Pattice

4 large potatoes

Salt to taste

Oil for shallow-frying

### Filling

1 cup split black gram (*dhuli urad dal*),
    soaked and boiled

1 tablespoon chopped fresh coriander
    leaves

2 green chillies, chopped

Black salt (*kala namak*) to taste

A pinch of asafoetida (*hing*)

½ inch ginger, chopped

½ teaspoon *chaat masala*

½ teaspoon red chilli powder

### Topping (one portion)

½ cup *matara* (dried yellow peas), bo

¼ cup yogurt

2 tablespoons Date and Tamarind
    Chutney (page 102)

½ tablespoon Green Coriander Chut
    (page100)

¼ teaspoon roasted cumin powder

¼ teaspoon *chaat masala*

¼ teaspoon red chilli powder

A few crisp, flat *puris* (*maide ki papd*
    crushed

## Method

1. Boil, peel and grate the potatoes. Put them into a bowl, add salt and mix.
2. In a separate bowl, combine the boiled *dhuli urad dal*, coriander leaves, green ch
    black salt, *hing*, ginger, *chaat masala* and chilli powder.
3. Knead the grated potatoes. Grease the palms of your hands. Place a portion of ma
    potato on one palm, flatten slightly, make a hollow in the centre and stuff with the f
    Enclose the filling with the potato and shape into a thick round *tikki*.
4. Heat the oil on a *tawa*; add the *tikki* and shallow-fry till golden brown on both sides
5. To serve, place each *pattice* on a plate. Flatten the centre slightly and place a few *m*
    in the hollow. Top with dollops of yogurt, date and tamarind chutney and green coria
    chutney. Sprinkle with cumin powder, *chaat masala* powder and chilli powder. Cru
    few *papdis* and sprinkle over the *chaat*. Serve immediately.

# FARALI CHAAT

*A feast (so tantalizingly chatpata) for a fasting day.*

## Ingredients

500 grams purple yam (*kand*), boiled and cut into small cubes

2–3 tablespoons pure *ghee*

1 teaspoon cumin seeds

3 green chillies, chopped

2 teaspoons red chilli powder

3 tablespoons chopped fresh coriander leaves

Rock salt (*sendha namak*) to taste

1½ cups yogurt, whisked and chilled

4 teaspoons Green Coriander Chutney (page 100)

4 teaspoons Date and Tamarind Chutney (page 102)

1 cup *farali chiwda*

## Method

1. Heat the ghee in a *kadai*; add the cumin seeds and sauté over a medium heat till they change colour.

2. Add the green chillies and sauté for half a minute. Add the *kand*, chilli powder, coriander leaves and rock salt and sauté for one minute, stirring and tossing continuously.

3. Transfer the mixture to four serving plates. Pour three or four tablespoons of chilled yogurt over each portion.

4. Drizzle one teaspoon each of green coriander chutney and date and tamarind chutney, sprinkle one-fourth cup of *farali chiwda* and serve immediately.

# FRUIT CHAAT

*Seasonal fruits all put together make a splendid sight indeed.*
*Try adding a few fresh mint leaves for those little bursts of freshness.*

## Ingredients

½ small papaya, cut into 1-inch cubes

2 kiwi fruits, cut into 1-inch cubes

½ cup pomegranate kernels

½ cup orange segments

½ cup sweet lime segments

1 medium apple, cut into 1-inch cubes

¼ cup seedless green grapes, halved

¼ cup seedless black grapes, halved

½ teaspoon red chilli powder

1 ½ tablespoons *chaat masala*

Rock salt (*sendha namak*) to taste

1 tablespoon lemon juice

## Method

1. Combine the papaya, kiwi fruit, pomegranate kernels, orange and sweet lime segments, apple and green and black grapes in a large bowl and place in a refrigerator to chill thoroughly.

2. Just before serving, sprinkle with chilli powder, *chaat masala* and rock salt. Add the lemon juice and toss gently to mix. Serve immediately.

# FRIED GARADU INDORI STYLE

*Garadu is a winter speciality in Indore and a popular street food especially at Sarafa near Rajwad*
*People throng there post–dinner, mind you, and feast on fried garadu, mawa baati (gulab jamuns) a.*
*bhutte ka kees (makai upma)!*

## Ingredients

700–800 grams *garadu* (see below)

Oil for deep-frying

2 tablespoons Jiralu Masala (see below)

Salt to taste

2 tablespoons lemon juice

2 tablespoons chopped fresh coriander leaves

## Method

1. Trim the narrow tapering ends of the *garadu* and use only the middle section. Grea
   knife and remove the peel. Cut *garadu* into large chunks.

2. Boil seven to eight cups of water in a deep pan. Add *garadu* chunks and boil till just d
   To check, insert a knife into the thickest part of the *garadu* after six to seven minutes
   goes in easily the *garadu* is cooked. Remove from heat and place in a colander to d
   Leave to cool completely.

3. Chop the *garadu* into small bite-sized squares. Heat the oil in a *kadai* over a high h
   Deep-fry the *garadu* till lightly coloured. Drain on absorbent paper.

4. Just before serving, refry the *garadu* in moderately hot oil till crisp. Drain on absor
   paper.

5. Divide the fried *garadu* equally between serving plates, sprinkle *jiralu masala* pow
   salt, lemon juice and coriander leaves and serve immediately.

**Note**: *Garadu* is a type of yam. It is somewhat like sweet potato (*ratalu*) in appearance.

To make Jiralu Masala, mix together 2 teaspoons roasted cumin powder, 1½ teaspoons dried
ginger powder (soonth), ½ teaspoon red chilli powder, ¼ teaspoon turmeric powder, a pinch
asafoetida (hing), ½ teaspoon black salt (*kala namak*), ½ teaspoon rock salt (*sendha namak*

# GREEN CHANA CHAAT

*Though best made with fresh green chana when in season, you can use the dried ones too.
Perk them up with spring onion greens and chopped paneer or tofu.*

## Ingredients

1½ cups dried green Bengal gram (*hara chana*), soaked overnight

2 medium onions, chopped

2 medium tomatoes, chopped

2–3 green chillies, chopped

2 tablespoons chopped fresh coriander leaves

Black salt (*kala namak*) to taste

1 teaspoon roasted cumin powder

1 teaspoon *chaat masala*

½ teaspoon red chilli powder

2 tablespoons lemon juice

## Method

1. Pressure-cook the soaked gram in three cups of water till the pressure is released tw
   three times (two or three whistles), or till tender.

2. Transfer the *chana* to a *kadai* and simmer till all the water evaporates.

3. Place the hot *chana* in a bowl. Add the onions, tomatoes, green chillies, coriander lea
   black salt, roasted cumin powder, *chaat masala*, chilli powder and lemon juice
   mix well.

4. Serve immediately

# HEALTHY CORNFLAKE BHEL

*What I like best about this bhel is that there is no fuss in preparing it.*

*I miss the green mango when not in season, but not so much that I would give this snack a miss*

## Ingredients

2 cups cornflakes

1 large potato, boiled and diced

1 medium onion, chopped

1 large cucumber, seeded and diced

1 large tomato, seeded and diced

1 cup pomegranate kernels

Salt to taste

1 teaspoon *chaat masala*

2 tablespoons unripe green mango, chopped

2 tablespoons chopped fresh coriander leaves

2 teaspoons lemon juice

## Method

1.  In a large bowl, combine the potato, onion, cucumber, tomato, pomegranate, salt, *masala* and green mango and toss well to mix.

2.  Add the cornflakes, coriander leaves and lemon juice and toss again to mix well.

3.  Transfer the *bhel* to a serving bowl and serve immediately.

# INSTANT DAHI WADE

*In this world of quick fixes, I would give this recipe an award!*
*It is truly delicious and if you don't tell, no one will guess the origin of the 'wade'!*

## Ingredients

8 large *jeera* butter biscuits
4 cups thin buttermilk
2½ cups yogurt, whisked and chilled
½ teaspoon rock salt (*sendha namak*)
1 teaspoon red chilli powder
1 teaspoon roasted cumin powder
½ cup Date and Tamarind Chutney (page 102)
¼ cup chopped fresh coriander leaves

## Method

1.  Soak the *jeera* biscuits in buttermilk for eight to ten minutes till soft. Drain, squeeze l
    between your palms and set aside. Alternatively, soak the biscuits in four cups of
    water for four or five minutes and drain.
2.  Place two soaked biscuits in each serving bowl, and pour chilled yogurt
    over the biscuits.
3.  Serve, garnished with rock salt, chilli powder, cumin powder, date and tamarind ch
    and coriander leaves.

# JHAAL MURI

*Jhaal is 'spicy' in Bengali and Muri is 'murmura'. Jhaal Muri is a popular street food in Kolkata.*
*If your chilli tolerance is high, go for more pickle oil and masala*
*because there are always rosogollas to follow!*

## Ingredients

2 cups puffed rice (*murmura*)

1 medium onion, chopped

¼ cup sprouted whole black gram (*kala chana*), boiled

1 small cucumber, cut into ½ -inch cubes

1 small tomato, seeded and cut into ½-inch cubes

2 green chillies, chopped

2 tablespoons roasted peanuts, skinned

2 tablespoons chopped fresh coriander leaves

2 tablespoons mustard oil (taken from a pickle)

2 tablespoons *Jhaal Muri Masala* (see below)

Fresh coconut, sliced, to garnish

## Method

1. In a large bowl, combine the puffed rice, onion, sprouted *kala chana*, cucumber, tomato, green chillies, peanuts, and coriander leaves and toss to mix well.
2. Add the mustard oil and *jhaal muri masala* and toss again to mix.
3. Serve immediately, garnished with sliced coconut.

### Notes:

- For the *Jhaal Muri Masala*, mix together 1 teaspoon rock salt (*sendha namak*), 1 tablespoon roasted cumin power, ½ tablespoon red chilli powder, 1 teaspoon *chaat masala* and ½ teaspoon white pepper powder.
- If you do not have a pickle containing mustard oil, heat 2 tablespoons of mustard oil in a pan to smoking point. Take it off the heat, add ½ teaspoon mustard seeds, ¼ teaspoon fenugreek seeds (*methi dana*), ¼ teaspoon fennel seeds (*saunf*), ½ teaspoon red chilli powder and a pinch of asafoetida (*hing*). Leave to stand for one hour, strain and use.

# KACHORI CHAAT

*Talk about a filling snack!*

*The kachoris are filled with a hefty stuffing and the toppings add their weight!*

*The kachoris taste better when served warm.*

## Ingredients

1 cup refined flour (*maida*)

¼ teaspoon carom seeds (*ajwain*)

¼ teaspoon salt

A pinch of soda bicarbonate

2 tablespoons pure *ghee*

### Filling

½ cup shelled green peas, lightly
   crushed

½ tablespoon oil + for deep-frying

A pinch of asafoetida (*hing*)

¼ teaspoon cumin seeds

½ inch ginger, chopped

2 green chillies, chopped

Salt to taste

¼ teaspoon *garam masala* powder

2 tablespoons grated coconut

2 tablespoons roasted peanuts, crushed

### Topping

2 cups yogurt, whisked and chilled

1 teaspoon red chilli powder

2 teaspoons roasted cumin powder

4 teaspoons Green Coriander Chutney
   (page 100)

4 teaspoons Date and Tamarind Chutney
   (page 102)

## Method

1. For the filling, heat the oil in a pan; add the asafoetida and cumin seeds. When the cumin seeds begin to change colour, add the ginger, green chillies, green peas and salt. Mix and cook for two or three minutes. Remove from heat and stir in the *garam masala* powder. Set aside to cool. When completely cold, add the coconut and peanuts and mix well.

2. For the *kachoris*, mix together the refined flour, carom seeds, salt, soda bicarbonate and pure ghee in a bowl. Add enough cold water and knead into a stiff dough.

3. Divide the dough into eight equal portions. Roll out each portion and press to make round *puris*. Stuff each *puri* with the stuffing and shape into a *kachori*.

4. Heat plenty of oil in a *kadai* and deep-fry the *kachoris* in moderately hot oil till crisp and golden. Drain on absorbent paper.

5. To serve, lightly crush two to three *kachoris* and place them in individual serving bowls. Pour some yogurt over, sprinkle chilli powder and cumin powder, drizzle both the chutneys and serve immediately.

# KARELA CHAAT

*When I first offered this chaat to my daughters they were turned off by the word karela!*
*But now it is a different story... they want me to cook these maida karelas as a vegetable so that*
*they can forego the real bitter ones!*

## Ingredients

2 cups refined flour (*maida*)

Salt to taste

8–10 black peppercorns, crushed

4 tablespoons *ghee*, melted

2 cups yogurt, whisked

2 teaspoons sugar

Oil for deep-frying

1 cup Green Coriander Chutney
    (page100)

Black salt (*kala namak*) to taste

2 medium boiled potatoes, cut into
    ½ -inch pieces

1 cup Date and Tamarind Chutney
    (page 102)

1 teaspoon red chilli powder

1 teaspoon roasted cumin powder

1 cup *sev*

2 tablespoons chopped fresh
    coriander leaves

## Method

1. Combine the flour, salt, crushed peppercorns and *ghee* in a bowl. Add some cold w
   and knead into a dough. Roll the dough out into thin sheets. Cover and set aside to
   for a while.

2. Combine the yogurt and sugar in a bowl. Strain and squeeze through a piece of mu
   into another bowl. Set aside.

3. To make the *karelas*, cut the rolled out dough into six-inch by four-inch rectangles. M
   small slits at even intervals and moisten the edges with water. Roll up the pieces
   press the edges together to seal.

4. Heat the oil till moderately hot in a *kadai*. Deep-fry the *karelas* till golden. Drair
   absorbent paper.

5. Place a couple of *karelas* on a plate. Top with yogurt, green coriander chutney, black
   potatoes, date and tamarind chutney, more yogurt, chilli powder, roasted cumin powder
   and coriander leaves. Garnish with a whole fried or crushed *karela*. Serve immediately

# KATORI CHAAT

*Potato baskets make excellent containers for many types of fillings but*
*potatoes have a special affinity for chole! Remember chole tikki...*

## Ingredients

5 medium potatoes

2 tablespoons oil + for deep-frying

*Chole* filling (page 24), as required

4 tablespoons thick yogurt

Date and Tamarind Chutney (page 102), as required

Green Coriander Chutney (page 100), as required

*Sev*, as required

2–3 tablespoons chopped fresh coriander leaves

## Method

1. Grate the potatoes and soak them in water for five minutes. Drain thoroughly and sp
   on absorbent kitchen paper to dry. Divide into four portions.
2. Take two small strainers – one slightly larger than the other.
3. Heat plenty of oil in a *kadai*. For each *katori*, layer the bigger strainer with one po
   of the grated potatoes. Place the other strainer over the potato layer and press lig
   Gently lower both the strainers together into the hot oil and deep-fry till golden. Drai
   absorbent paper and set aside.
4. Fill the *chole* in each of the fried *katoris*. Drizzle one tablespoon of yogurt over each.
   with date and tamarind chutney and green coriander chutney. Sprinkle *sev* and coria
   leaves and serve immediately.

# KHASTA ALOO CHAAT

*If you want to add glamour to a tikki, make it the way it is described here.*
*The chutney within is a real surprise and the clincher is the*
*complementary flavours of the other two chutneys.*

## Ingredients

4 large potatoes, boiled and mashed

Salt to taste

2 tablespoons cornflour

Oil for deep-frying

½ cup thick Green Coriander Chutney (page 100)

4–5 tablespoons arrowroot flour

1 tablespoon Red Chilli-Garlic Chutney (page 101)

4–5 tablespoons Date and Tamarind Chutney (page 102)

1 teaspoon *chaat masala*

## Method

1.  In a large bowl, combine the potatoes with salt and cornflour and mix well. Divide
    potato mixture into sixteen equal portions and shape into lemon-sized balls.

2.  Flatten a portion of mashed potato on your palm and place one teaspoon of g
    coriander chutney in the centre. Bring the sides together to enclose the filling and s
    into small squares. Dust with a little arrowroot flour and set aside.

3.  Heat the oil in a *kadai* and deep-fry the squares, a few at a time, till golden brown. [
    on absorbent paper.

4.  Place the fried potato squares on individual serving plates, drizzle with red chilli-
    chutney and date and tamarind chutney, sprinkle *chaat masala* and serve immediate

# KOTHIMBIR WADI CHAAT

*Kothimbir wadi is always served with a chutney as it is a dry snack.*
*I have enhanced the presentation with the addition of dahi...*
*serve immediately because the wadi should remain crisp.*

## Ingredients

1 cup chopped fresh coriander leaves

1 cup gram flour (*besan*)

4 green chillies, chopped

2 teaspoons grated jaggery

Salt to taste

A pinch of soda bicarbonate

½ teaspoon turmeric powder

2 tablespoons oil + for deep-frying

**To serve**

1½ cups *farsan*

1½ cups yogurt, whisked

4 tablespoons Green Coriander Chutney (page 100)

1 teaspoon *chaat masala*

2 tablespoons chopped fresh coriander leaves

## Method

1.  Combine one cup of coriander leaves, the gram flour, green chillies, jaggery, salt, bicarbonate, turmeric powder and two tablespoons of oil in a deep bowl. Add en water to make a thick batter.

2.  Pour the batter into a greased tray. Place the tray in a pressure cooker or a steame steam over high heat for fifteen to twenty minutes or till firm and cooked. Remove, and cut into one-inch cubes.

3.  Heat plenty of oil in a *kadai* and deep-fry the *kothimbir wadi* till light golden brown crisp. Drain on absorbent paper.

4.  To serve, divide the *wadi* between four individual bowls, top with *farsan*, drizzle s yogurt and green coriander chutney over and sprinkle with *chaat masala* and coria leaves. Serve immediately.

# MAKAI KA CHIWDA CHAAT

*Instant delights like this chaat come in handy when the kids demand something 'right now'!*
*Or add it to your list of recipes for unexpected guests.*

## Ingredients

2 cups *makai* ka *chiwda*

1 large potato, boiled, peeled and diced

1 medium onion, chopped

1 large cucumber, seeded and diced

1 large tomato, seeded and diced

2 tablespoons chopped unripe green mango

Salt to taste

1 green chilli, chopped

1 teaspoon *chaat masala*

2 teaspoons lemon juice

2 tablespoons chopped fresh coriander leaves

¼ cup sliced fresh coconut

## Method

1.  In a large bowl, combine the potato, onion, cucumber, tomato, green mango, salt, green chilli and *chaat masala* and toss to mix well.

2.  Add the *makai ka chiwda*, lemon juice and toss again to mix.

3.  Transfer to a serving bowl. Garnish with coriander leaves and coconut slices and serve immediately.

# MASALA DOSA CHAAT

*Accept the compliments that come your way for this creative snack!*
*Ensure that the ragda is warm. I suggest you do not stint on the red chilli–garlic chutney*
*because that is what adds maximum punch.*

## Ingredients

2 cups *dosa* batter

Red Chilli-Garlic Chutney (page 101),
  as required

1½ cups potato *bhaji*, lightly mashed

2 large onions, chopped

2 large tomatoes, chopped

1 teaspoon red chilli powder

1½ teaspoons *chaat masala*

Oil for shallow-frying

2 tablespoons chopped fresh
coriander leaves

**Ragda**

½ cup dried white peas (*vatana*),
  soaked overnight

¼ teaspoon turmeric powder

A pinch of asafoetida (*hing*)

Salt to taste

2 teaspoons *chaat masala*

2 teaspoons Date and Tamarind Chutney
  (page 102)

## Method

1. For the *ragda*, pressure-cook *vatana* in three cups of water with turmeric powder, asafoetida and salt till the pressure is released four or five times (four or five whistles), or till soft. Mash the peas slightly. Add the *chaat masala* and date and tamarind chutney and a little water if too thick and simmer for ten minutes. Keep the *ragda* hot.

2. Heat and season a *dosa tawa*. Place a small ladleful of *dosa* batter on the *tawa* and spread evenly to make an eight-inch diameter dosa. Drizzle half a teaspoon of oil around the *dosa* and cook over a low heat for half a minute.

3. Spread a little chilli-garlic chutney all over the *dosa*. Sprinkle with some onions, tomatoes, chilli powder and *chaat masala*. Place a small portion of potato *bhaji* in the centre. Press gently with the back of a ladle till lightly mashed and spread all over the *dosa*. Drizzle some more oil and cook over a low heat so that the underside turns golden and crisp.

4. Roll the *dosa* up tightly like a spring roll, transfer onto a plate and cut into equal lengths and arrange on a serving platter.

5. Spoon *ragda* generously over the *dosa*, garnish with coriander leaves and serve hot.

# MASALA KHICHIA PAPAD

*This is something exclusive as it is a roadside treat in western parts of the country.
It's a simple papad made glorious with chutneys... something that can be rustled up at home at
moment's notice. Marwaris make their own khichia and usually serve it as a snack: roasted crisp w.
blackened edges and drizzled quite liberally with pure ghee and chilli powder.*

## Ingredients

8 *khichia papad*

8 teaspoons butter

4 tablespoons Green Coriander Chutney (page 100)

2 tablespoons Red Chilli-Garlic Chutney (page 101)

2 tablespoons *chaat masala*

4–5 tablespoons chopped fresh coriander leaves

## Method

1. Dry-roast all the *khichia papad* till crisp.
2. Drizzle one teaspoon of butter over each *papad* and top with dollops of the chutney
3. Sprinkle *chaat masala* and coriander leaves and serve immediately before the p
   becomes soggy.

# MASALA SANDWICH DOUBLE ROTI CHAAT

*I enjoy this more if the sandwich is toasted to a crisp on both sides. And yes, serve warm.*

## Ingredients

8 *pav*

4 medium potatoes, boiled and mashed

2 teaspoons oil

½ teaspoon mustard seeds

1 teaspoon red chilli powder

¼ teaspoon turmeric powder

½ teaspoon *garam masala* powder

Salt to taste

3–4 tablespoons butter

4 tablespoons Green Coriander Chutney (page 100)

4 tablespoons Date and Tamarind Chutney (page 102)

1 medium onion, chopped

8 tablespoons *sev*

4 tablespoons chopped fresh coriander leaves

## Method

1. Heat the oil in a pan; add the mustard seeds. When they begin to splutter, add mashed potatoes, chilli powder, turmeric powder, *garam masala* powder and salt.

2. Mix well and cook for three or four minutes. Remove and set aside.

3. Slit two *pav* horizontally, but do not cut through to separate the halves. Spread s butter on the insides of the *pav*. Stuff with the potato mixture and lightly toast the pa a *tawa* using a little butter.

4. Arrange two roasted *pav* on each serving plate. Top with green coriander chutney, and tamarind chutney, onion and a generous helping of *sev*. Garnish with coria leaves and serve immediately.

# MATHRI SEV PURI

*This takes fusion food to the next level: Punjabi mathris with Mexican salsa.*
*This will generate encores, so be prepared!*

## Ingredients

16 *mathri*

1 tablespoon oil

1 medium onion, chopped

1 cup American sweet corn, boiled

2 fresh red chillies, chopped

¼ cup sweet chilli sauce

½ teaspoon *chaat masala*

1 tablespoon chopped fresh mint leaves

2 tablespoons chopped fresh coriander leaves

Salt to taste

1 tablespoon lemon juice

½ cup *sev*

2 tablespoons chopped fresh parsley

## Method

1. Heat the oil in a pan; add the onions and sauté till translucent. Add the corn and s
   for half a minute. Add the fresh red chillies, sweet chilli sauce and toss to mix. Add
   *chaat masala*, mint leaves and coriander leaves and salt. Mix and cook till dry.
2. Stir in the lemon juice. Divide the mixture into sixteen portions. Place each portion
   *mathri*. Sprinkle *sev*, garnish with parsley and serve immediately.

# MEXICAN CHAAT

*Succulent corn kernels are just perfect teamed up with the crunch of the corn chips in this chaat.*
*I prefer to add more green coriander chutney than the sweet one.*

## Ingredients

25–30 tortilla or corn chips, crushed

1 cup corn kernels, boiled

2 medium potatoes, boiled and chopped

1 large onion, chopped

1 large tomato, chopped

1 jalapeño chilli, chopped

2–3 tablespoons Green Coriander Chutney (page 100)

3–4 tablespoons Date and Tamarind Chutney (page 102)

Salt to taste

1 cup yogurt, whisked and chilled

1 tablespoon chopped fresh coriander leaves

## Method

1. Chill the yogurt in a refrigerator.
2. In a large bowl, combine the crushed corn chips (reserving some for garnishing), c
   potatoes, onion, tomato, jalapeño chilli, two tablespoons of green coriander chu
   three tablespoons of date and tamarind chutney and salt; toss well to mix.
3. Add the chilled yogurt and mix well with a spoon or a spatula.
4. Transfer the mixture to a platter, drizzle the remaining green coriander chutney and
   and tamarind chutney on top, and serve, garnished with the reserved corn chips and
   coriander leaves.

# PAANI PURI

*Call it 'puchka', 'gol gappe', 'pani patasa' or 'paani puri', the joy of this very Indian snack is now spreading across the world! I have experimented with various fillings including prawn balchao!*

## Ingredients

40 crisp puffed *puris*

1½ cups Date and Tamarind Chutney (page 102)

**Filling**

1 cup bean (*moong*) sprouts, boiled

2 large boiled potatoes cut into
¼ -inch cubes

Black salt (*kala namak*) to taste

1 teaspoon *chaat masala*

**Paani**

1 small bunch (25 grams) fresh
coriander leaves, chopped

1 small bunch (30 grams) fresh mint
leaves, chopped

5–6 green chillies

2 tablespoons *paani puri masala*

½ tablespoon dried mango
powder (*amchur*)

Black salt (*kala namak*) to taste

Salt to taste

½ tablespoon roasted cumin powder

3 tablespoons lemon juice

¼ cup *boondi*

## Method

1. To make the sprout filling, combine all the ingredients in a bowl, toss to mix well and set aside.

2. To make the *paani*, grind the coriander leaves, mint leaves and green chillies with enough water to a paste. Transfer the ground paste to a large bowl, add the *paani puri masala*, dried mango powder, black salt, salt, cumin powder and lemon juice and stir to mix well. Stir in six cups of water and place in a refrigerator to chill.

3. Just before serving, stir in the *boondi*.

4. To serve, press down on the top of each *puri* with your thumb to make a holllow, fill with a little *moong* and potato filling followed by a half a tablespoon of date and tamarind chutney. Dip the *puri* in the prepared *paani* and serve immediately.

**Note**: For the *paani*, use 2–3 tablespoons of unripe green mango paste instead of lemon juice.

# PALAK PAKORE KI CHAAT

*When I first made this chaat, I was a little perplexed, as there was no reaction from the guests.*
*I thought they had not liked it! But then they asked if there was more and*
*I knew they were too stunned to comment... this chaat is really one of my favourite snacks!*

## Ingredients

16–20 fresh medium-sized spinach leaves (*palak*)

1½ cups coarse gram flour (*besan*)

Salt to taste

½ teaspoon red chilli powder

¼ teaspoon turmeric powder

½ teaspoon carom seeds (*ajwain*)

A pinch of asafoetida (*hing*)

Oil for deep-frying

1 cup yogurt

2 teaspoons roasted cumin seed powder

4 tablespoons Green Coriander Chutney (page 100)

4 tablespoons Date and Tamarind Chutney (page 102)

3 medium onions, chopped

½ cup *sev*

½ cup chopped fresh coriander leaves

## Method

1. In a bowl, combine the *besan*, salt, chilli powder, turmeric powder, carom seeds and asafoetida. Add sufficient water to make a thin batter.

2. Heat the oil in a *kadai*. Coat each spinach leaf with batter on both sides and deep-fry till golden brown and crisp. Drain on absorbent paper.

3. Whisk yogurt with salt to taste.

4. For each serving, place two *pakore* on a plate. Cover with two or three tablespoons of whisked yogurt and sprinkle with cumin powder. Top with dollops of green coriander chutney and date and tamarind chutney.

5. Sprinkle some chopped onions and cover liberally with *sev*. Garnish with coriander leaves and serve immediately.

# PAPDI CHAAT

*If you wish you can make the papdis at home.*

*To save tlme, cut into neat one–and–a–half inch squares.*

*A healthy version is to make the dough using one part refined flour and one part wheat flour.*

## Ingredients

20 crisp flat *puris* (*maide ki papdi*)

2 medium potatoes, boiled and sliced

1 large onion, sliced

2–3 tablespoons Date and Tamarind Chutney (page 102)

2 tablespoons Green Coriander Chutney (page 100)

1 teaspoon lemon juice

1 teaspoon roasted cumin powder

1 teaspoon *chaat masala*

½ teaspoon rock salt (*sendha namak*)

¼ cup yogurt, whisked and chilled

1 cup *sev*

2 tablespoons pomegranate kernels

2 tablespoons chopped fresh coriander leaves

## Method

1.  Arrange the *papdi* on a serving dish. Place a potato slice on each *papdi* and then top
    a slice of onion. Drizzle date and tamarind chutney and green coriander chutney on
    *papdi*.

2.  Sprinkle the lemon juice, cumin powder, *chaat masala* and rock salt over the *papo*
    drizzle some yogurt over.

3.  Top with the *sev*, pomegranate kernels and coriander leaves and serve immediately

# PAPDI PIZZA

*These attractive baby pizzas make super starters at a party.*
*You can put large batches under the grill! Kids too love them as an anytime treat.*

## Ingredients

20 flat crisp *puris* (*maide ki papdi*)

1 large onion

¼ cup pizza sauce

2 medium potatoes, boiled and sliced

¾ cup grated mozzarella cheese

2 medium green capsicums, sliced horizontally

Nylon *sev* as required

## Method

1. Preheat the oven to 180°C/350°F/Gas Mark 4.
2. Cut the onion into thick round slices and separate the rings.
3. Grease a baking tray and arrange the *papdis* on it.
4. Spread the pizza sauce on the *papdis*. Place potato slices on some *papdi* and o
   rings on the rest.
5. Place the grated cheese in small heaps on each *papdi* and place green capsicum s
   on some of them. Sprinkle with nylon sev. Put a little pizza sauce on top of some
   of the *papdi* pizzas.
6. Bake in the preheated oven till the cheese melts. Serve hot.

# PEANUT CHAAT

*This recipe is a contribution from Alyona, whose friend had served it at a kitty party.*
*The only time–consuming part is the peeling of the peanuts, otherwise it is a quick recipe.*
*And it is a unique one for sure!*

## Ingredients

2 cups raw peanuts

1 tablespoon sea salt

1 teaspoon turmeric powder

Salt to taste

¼ teaspoon *chaat masala*

½ teaspoon red chilli powder

1 teaspoon roasted cumin powder

1 medium onion, chopped

1 medium tomato, chopped

2 green chillies, chopped

2 tablespoons chopped fresh coriander leaves

2 tablespoons lemon juice

## Method

1. Pressure-cook the peanuts in five cups of water with sea salt and turmeric powd
   the pressure is released four or five times (four or five whistles). Drain and she
   peanuts.
2. Place the peanuts in a bowl. Add the salt, *chaat masala*, chilli powder, roasted c
   powder, onion, tomato, green chillies, coriander leaves, and lemon juice and mix we
3. Serve hot or cold.

# RAGDA PATTICE

*What is popular as 'chole tikki' in the north takes on this form in the western and central part of* *country. I prefer to make the ragda a little runny as it thickens on cooling. Some people like to temp* *with tomatoes and garam masala, but plain and simple is just as nice.*

## Ingredients

1¼ cups dried white peas (*vatana*)

4 large potatoes, boiled, peeled and mashed

¼ teaspoon turmeric powder

A pinch asafoetida (*hing*)

Salt to taste

2 tablespoons cornflour

2–3 green chillies, chopped

Oil for shallow-frying

Green Coriander Chutney (page 100), as required

Date and Tamarind Chutney (page 102), as required

2 medium onions, chopped

2 teaspoons *chaat masala*

2 tablespoons chopped fresh coriander leaves

## Method

1.  Soak the dried peas in three cups of water for about six hours. Drain and boil in or four cups of water with turmeric powder, asafoetida and salt till soft. Mash the slightly. Add a little water if too thick and simmer for ten minutes. Keep the *ragda* ho

2.  Add the cornflour, green chillies and salt to the mashed potato and mix well. Divide eight equal portions, shape into balls and flatten slightly into *pattice*.

3.  Heat a little oil in a frying pan and fry the *pattice* gently on both sides over a medium till evenly browned. Keep warm.

4.  To serve, place two *pattice* on a plate and spoon some *ragda* over.

5.  Drizzle green coriander chutney and date and tamarind chutney over the top and sp with onion, *chaat masala* and coriander leaves. Serve immediately.

# RAJ KACHORI WITH CHOLE

*The kachori in this recipe is somewhat special. It can take a little practice to work with semolina dough but the effort is absolutely worth it. This is something that can impress even the fussiest of guests.*
*Or better still, make it when you invite the boss for high tea!*

## Ingredients

¼ cup semolina (*sooji/rawa*)

2 tablespoons refined flour (*maida*)

¼ teaspoon red chilli powder

Salt to taste

Oil for deep-frying

### Filling

2 tablespoons gram flour (*besan*)

A pinch of soda bicarbonate

¼ teaspoon red chilli powder

Salt to taste

¼ teaspoon fennel (*saunf*) powder

A pinch of black pepper powder

1½ tablespoons oil

### Topping

1 cup Chole Filling (page 24)

1 cup yogurt, whisked

½ cup Date and Tamarind Chutney
   (page 102)

2 tablespoons Green Coriander Chutney
   (page 100)

1 teaspoon roasted cumin powder

½ teaspoon rock salt (*sendha namak*)

1 teaspoon red chilli powder

½ cup sev

2–3 tablespoons chopped fresh
   coriander leaves

## Method

1. Make a stiff dough of semolina, refined flour, chilli powder, salt and water. Mix together gram flour, soda bicarbonate, chilli powder, salt, fennel powder, black pepper powder and oil. Add sufficient water and knead into a dough.

2. Divide both the semolina dough and the gram flour dough into four equal parts each. Spread each portion of the semolina dough on your palm and place one portion of the gram flour dough in the centre. Gather the edges and shape into a ball. Further roll into a *kachori*.

3. Heat the oil in a *kadai* and deep-fry the *kachoris* over medium heat, turning once, till puffed up and crisp. Drain on absorbent paper and leave to cool. If they soften when cool, deep-fry again.

4. To serve, place each *kachori* on a serving plate. Make a large hole in the centre and fill with a generous portion of *chole*. Pour one-fourth cup of yogurt over, and top with dollops of both the chutneys. Sprinkle cumin powder, rock salt, chilli powder, *sev* and coriander leaves over everything. Serve immediately.

# SAMOSA CHOLE

*Ideal for a filling rainy–day snack.*
*Control the spice in the chole if your tolerance level is low.*

## Ingredients

4 *samosas*

Chole Filling (page 24), as required

4 tablespoons yogurt, whisked

4 tablespoons Date and Tamarind Chutney (page 102)

4 tablespoons Green Coriander Chutney (page 100)

## Method

1. To serve, place the *samosas* on a serving platter, crush lightly and top with a generous portion of the *chole*.

2. Pour yogurt over the *chole*, drizzle date and tamarind chutney and green coriander chutney and serve hot.

# SEV BATATA PURI

*As popular as bhel puri and paani puri on the roadside!*
*It makes an ideal starter at a party as there is only last minute assembling required.*

## Ingredients

24 crisp flat *puris* (*maide ki papdi*)

2 large potatoes, boiled, peeled and chopped

1 small green unripe mango, chopped

Salt to taste

¼ teaspoon red chilli powder

2 medium onions, chopped

¼ cup Green Coriander Chutney (page 100)

2 tablespoons Red Chilli-Garlic Chutney (page 101)

¼ cup Date and Tamarind Chutney (page 102)

1 cup *sev*

½ tablespoon *chaat masala*

2 tablespoons chopped coriander leaves

## Method

1. Arrange the *puris* on a plate.
2. Mix together the potatoes, green mango, salt and chilli powder.
3. Place portions of the mixture on the *puris*. Sprinkle the onion over the potato mixtu
4. Drizzle green coriander chutney, red chilli-garlic chutney and date and tamarind ch over the top.
5. Cover the *puris* with plenty of *sev*.
6. Sprinkle *chaat masala* and coriander leaves and serve immediately.

# TAWA PANEER CHAAT

*When it comes to filling the puri with something different, paneer is a good choice, especially with al[...]
masala and spice.*

## Ingredients

500 grams cottage cheese (*paneer*), cut into ½ -inch pieces

Crisp puffed *puris* (as for *paani puri*)

3 tablespoons oil

2 large onions, chopped

1 teaspoon ginger paste

1 teaspoon garlic paste

3–4 green chillies, seeded and chopped

¾ cup tomato purée

3–4 tablespoons *pav bhaji masala*

Salt to taste

½ tablespoon *chaat masala*

2-3 tablespoons chopped fresh coriander leaves

## Method

1. Heat the oil on a *tawa*; add the onions and sauté till brown. Add the ginger paste [...] garlic paste and continue to sauté for a few minutes.

2. Add a little water and continue to sauté for one minute. Add the green chillies and s[...] for another minute.

3. Add the tomato purée, *pav bhaji masala*, salt and *chaat masala* and continue to [...] over a low heat till the oil separates from the *masala*.

4. Add the cubed *paneer* and half the coriander leaves and stir gently to mix. C[...] seasoning and cook over a low heat for two minutes.

5. Make small holes in each *puri* and stuff with the *paneer* mixture. Serve, garnished wit[...] remaining coriander leaves.

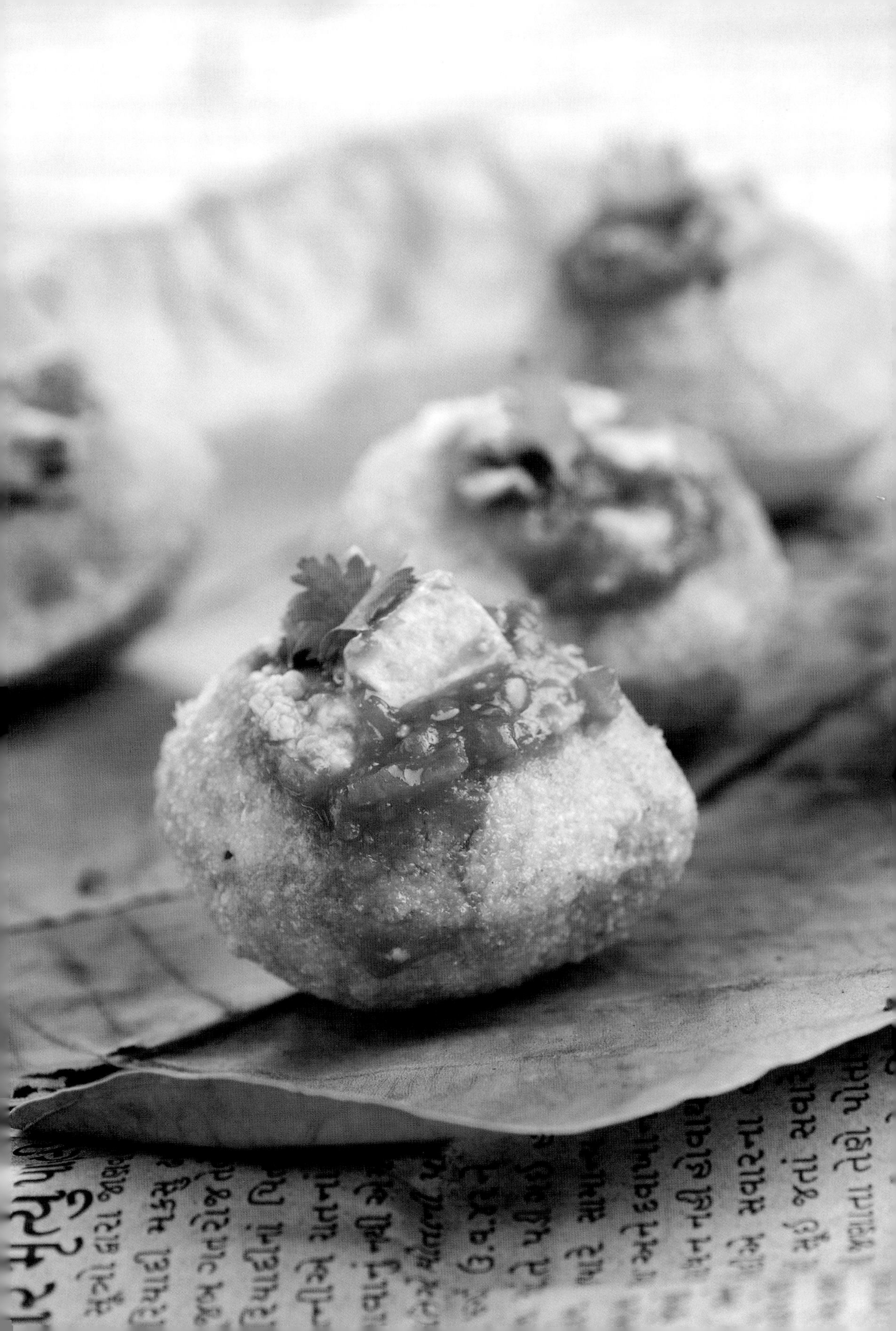

# URAD DAL PAPAD CHAAT

*This is a version of the masala papad often served in Indian restaurants.*
*You can pre-roast the papads and store in an airtight container.*

## Ingredients

10 large *urad dal papads*
2 teaspoons oil
¼ teaspoon mustard seeds
A pinch of asafoetida (*hing*)
1 large onion, chopped
1 medium cucumber, seeded and chopped
1 medium tomato, seeded and chopped
3 tablespoons chopped fresh coriander leaves
2 teaspoons *chaat masala*
2 teaspoons lemon juice
1 teaspoon Red Chilli-Garlic Chutney (page 101)

## Method

1. Roast the *papads* on a *tawa* over a low heat pressing lightly with a piece of muslin. V
   slightly cool, crush into fine pieces with your fingers and place in a bowl and set as
2. Heat the oil in a pan; add the mustard seeds and asafoetida. When the seeds beg
   splutter, remove from heat and pour onto the crushed *papads* and toss well.
3. Mix together the onion, cucumber, tomato, half the coriander leaves, *chaat masala*, le
   juice and chilli-garlic chutney and toss with the *papad* mixture.
4. Garnish with the remaining coriander leaves and serve immediately.

# GREEN CORIANDER CHUTNEY

## Ingredients

1 cup fresh coriander leaves

½ cup fresh mint leaves

2–3 green chillies, seeded and chopped

Black salt (*kala namak*) to taste

¼ teaspoon sugar

1 teaspoon lemon juice

## Method

1. Clean, wash and roughly chop coriander and mint leaves.
2. In a blender, process chopped coriander and mint leaves with chopped green chil
   Make a smooth paste using a little water if required.
3. Add black salt and sugar and blend again.
4. Transfer to a bowl and stir in the lemon juice.

# RED CHILLI-GARLIC CHUTNEY

## Ingredients

10 dried red chillies, seeded

12 large cloves garlic, peeled and chopped

2 teaspoons lemon juice

Sea salt to taste

1 teaspoon cumin powder

## Method

1. Soak red chillies in one and a half cups of water for half an hour. Drain.
2. Grind the red chillies and garlic cloves with lemon juice to a fine paste. Add a little water if necessary.
3. Add sea salt and cumin powder and mix well.

# DATE AND TAMARIND CHUTNEY

## Ingredients

15–20 dates (*khajoor*)

1 cup tamarind pulp

2 teaspoons cumin seeds

¼ teaspoon fennel seeds (*saunf*)

½ cup grated jaggery

2 teaspoons red chilli powder

1 teaspoon dried ginger powder (*soonth*)

1 teaspoon black salt (*sendha namak*)

Salt to taste

## Method

1. Wash, stone dates and chop roughly.
2. Dry-roast cumin seeds and fennel seeds. Cool slightly, and grind together to a powd
3. Mix together dates, jaggery, tamarind pulp, cumin and fennel powders, chilli pow
   dried ginger powder, black salt, salt to taste and four cups of water.
4. Cook over a medium heat till it comes to a boil. Lower the heat and continue to coo
   six to eight minutes.
5. Cool and serve.

**UY NOW!**

# Titles by *Sanjeev Kapoor* from *Popular Prakashan*

*"My books are not simply a collection of recipes but an attempt to encourage people to cook... and cook with confidence"*

| Title | MRP ₹ |
|---|---|
| Mithai - Sweet for every celebration | 295 |
| Cooking with Love - Vegetarian Recipes from My Mother's Kitchen | 295 |
| Healthy Indian Cooking for Diabetes | 345 |
| 100 Favourite Hand-Picked Recipes | 595 |
| Fun Food for Fussy Kids | 350 |
| Simply Stylish Entertaining at Home | 395 |
| Wedding Collection - Recipes for Newly-weds | 1200 |
| Dakshin Delights | 295 |
| Everyday Indian with Olive Oil | 495 |
| Marwari Vegetarian Cooking | 295 |
| Tandoori Cooking @ Home | 275 |
| Flavours of the Orient | 250 |
| Wrap 'N' Roll | 350 |
| TV Dinners | 350 |
| Party Cooking | 295 |
| Chaat | 350 |
| Dal and Kadhi | 350 |
| Cakes and Bakes | 295 |
| Royal Hyderabadi Cooking | 350 |
| No-Oil Vegetarian Cooking | 275 |
| No-Oil Cooking | 295 |
| Konkan Cookbook | 275 |
| Simply Indian | 275 |
| Best of Chinese Cooking | 275 |
| Microwave Cooking Made Easy | 295 |
| Khazana of Healthy Tasty Recipes | 250 |
| Any Time Temptations | 295 |
| Low Calorie Vegetarian Cookbook | 295 |
| Khana Khazana: Celebration of Indian Cookery | 295 |
| Khazana of Indian Vegetarian Recipes | 275 |
| Khazana of Indian Recipes | 295 |

**Everyday Cooking**
...ana for Delicious Dailies
MRP ₹ 295/-

**Low-Salt Cookbok**
MRP ₹ 195/-

**Tiffins**
Delicious and Healthy
Khana for Dabba
MRP ₹ 295/-

**The Yellow Chilli Cookbook**
MRP ₹ 595/-

**Chocolate**
MRP ₹ 595/-

**TURN OVER** for more books by Sanjeev Kapoor

# More Titles by Sanjeev Kapoor from Popular Prakashan

| | MRP ₹ | | MRP ₹ |
|---|---|---|---|
| ➢ The Party Food Cookbook | 110 | ➢ Noodles and Pasta | 110 |
| ➢ Non-Vegetarian Soups and Salads | 99 | ➢ Makai Magic | 99 |
| ➢ Best of Paneer: A Collection of Vegetarian Recipes | 99 | ➢ Eggs | 99 |
| ➢ Cocktails Snacks | 99 | ➢ Desi Aloo | 99 |
| ➢ Desi Murgh | 99 | ➢ Dahi | 125 |
| ➢ Curries | 99 | ➢ Rice, Biryani and Pulao | 125 |
| ➢ South Indian Snacks | 99 | ➢ Vegetarian Rice, Biryani and Pulao | 125 |
| ➢ Roti-Paranthe | 110 | ➢ Kadai Cooking | 110 |
| ➢ Vegetarian Breakfast Bonanza | 125 | ➢ Pressure Cooking | 99 |
| ➢ Scrumptious Vegetarian Salads | 99 | ➢ No-Oil Recipes | 99 |
| ➢ Delicious Vegetarian Soups | 99 | ➢ No-Oil Vegetarian Recipes | 110 |
| ➢ Vegetarian After-School Snacks | 125 | ➢ Street Food | 125 |
| ➢ Vegetarian Soups | 125 | ➢ Desi Mutton | 95 |
| ➢ Recipes for Non-Stick Cookware | 125 | ➢ Thai Cooking | 99 |
| ➢ Vegetarian Cooking with Dahi | 110 | ➢ Paneer | 110 |
| ➢ Go Green | 99 | ➢ Italian Cooking | 99 |
| ➢ Kitchen Library Vegetarian Collection (set of 5 volumes) | 485 | ➢ Drinks and Mocktails | 125 |
| | | ➢ Vegetarian Breakfasts | 125 |
| ➢ Healthy Tasty Recipes | 99 | ➢ Salads | 125 |
| ➢ Monsoon Medley | 99 | ➢ Non-Vegetarian Recipes From Around The World | 99 |
| ➢ Chill Out! Summer Eats & Treats | 99 | ➢ Vegetarian Recipes From Around The World | 110 |
| ➢ Mango Masti | 99 | | |
| ➢ Tawa-Handi Recipes | 125 | ➢ Seafood | 125 |
| ➢ Sunday Specials | 125 | ➢ Chicken Recipes | 125 |
| ➢ Simple Home Baking | 99 | ➢ Punjabi | 99 |
| ➢ Chai-Nashta | 125 | ➢ Chinese Non-Vegetarian Cooking | 110 |
| ➢ Mirch Mazaa | 125 | ➢ Chinese Vegetarian Cooking | 99 |
| ➢ Sweet Temptations | 110 | ➢ Microwave Desi Cooking | 110 |
| ➢ Dal-Roti | 99 | ➢ Sweet Encounters | 99 |
| ➢ Desi Sabziyan | 110 | ➢ Soups, Salads and Sandwiches | 110 |
| ➢ Pickles, Chutneys 'n' More | 110 | ➢ Vegetarian Snacks and Starters | 110 |
| ➢ Say Cheese! | 99 | ➢ Non-Vegetarian Snacks and Starters | 110 |
| ➢ Mushroom Mania | 99 | | |

## New Releases books

**Iron-Rich Recipes**
MRP ₹ 110/-

**Vegetarian Finger Foods**
MRP ₹ 110/-

**Kabab Lajawab!**
MRP ₹ 99/-

**Vegetarian Recipes From Marwar**
MRP ₹ 99/-

**Noodles & Rice**
MRP ₹ 99/-

## Set of 5 books

Kitchen Library Eat Lite
Low-calorie
Vegetarian Collection
**MRP ₹ 485/-**

=

Beverages
Soups & Salads

Snacks & Starters

Main Dishes

Accompaniments

Sweets & Desserts

## ORDER NOW!

Contact the address below or visit our we
www.popularprakshan.com and www.sanjeevkapo

Popular Prakashan
www.popularprakashan.com

For further enquiries contact:
**Popular Prakashan Pvt. Ltd.** 301, Mahalaxmi Chambers, 22, Bhulabhai Desai Road, Mumbai 400
Phone: 022-23530303 • Fax: 022-23535294 • E-mail: info@popularprakashan.com